Get the Deed!
"Subject-To"
The Existing Financing

Copyright © 2014, 2015, 2016, 2021 by Alicia A. Cox,

All rights reserved. This book or any portion may not be reproduced or used in any manner whatsoever without the express written permission by the author, except for the use of brief quotations in a book review.

Published by: CashFlow Systems
Oceanside, CA
www.mycashflowuniversity.com

Printed in the United States of America

Library of Congress Control Number: 2021902679
ISBN 978-1-7366658-0-0

Disclaimer: The information provided here is meant to give information on the subject covered. This information was gathered from actual experiences and the information is not meant to give legal advice. Laws and practices vary from state to state and the subject discussed changes according to new laws. Since information is always changing and each situation might be different, the reader is advised to consult with his or her own legal, accounting and consulting professional.

The author has taken reasonable precautions in the preparation of the information presented in this book and believes the information presented herein is accurate as of the date produced. Author assumes no responsibility for any errors or omissions. The Author further disclaims any liability resulting from the use or application of the information contained in this book.

This information is not intended to give or serve as legal advice.

DEDICATION

To the Lord and Savior of my life Jesus Christ, Son of The Highest God, thank you for helping me to realize my dream of becoming a full-time real estate investor.

To the members of The Antelope Valley Real Estate Investors Association 2013-2014

Thank you for your faithful support and love.

"Make **It** happen.
Don't let sh**It** happen to you!"
    -ALICIA COX

Get the Deed!
"Subject-To"
The Existing Financing

How to Get Rich Buying and Selling Houses... No Cash, No Credit, No Banks, No Kidding

ALICIA A. COX

Contents

Introduction	1
1_Get the Deed to Beautiful Homes	5
How Much Money Can You Make?	9
2_What is "Subject-To" Investing?	13
Why Would a Seller Sell Subject-To?	19
3_The "Subject-To" Secret	23
Secret #1 Ownership & Debt.	23
Secret #2 You're a Problem Solver	24
Secret #3 Offer a Solution	24
Secret #4 Got Problems?	25
Secret #5 Why it Works	25
4_How to Find Motivated Sellers	27
Getting Motivated Sellers to Call You	28
5_How to Get the Deed	35
The Purchase Agreement	37
The Subject-To Deal Sheet	40
6_The Art of Closing the Deal	41
What to Do After You Take Over Title	44

7 The Exit Strategy Finding Buyers	47
Filling Your Homes Super-Fast	*50*
8 Creative Techniques to Building Wealth	53
Creating Unlimited Cash Flow	*55*
9 The Due on Sale Clause	61
Working with The Lender	*62*
Negotiating Liens with Lien Holders	*63*
10 Working with Sellers in Foreclosure	67
Frequently Asked Questions	73
Epilogue	79
Deal Killers, When You Have to Back Out	*79*
Next Steps….	83
About the Author	100

INTRODUCTION

I have been a real estate investor now for over 20 years as of the date of this publishing. During that time, I have bought, flipped, rehabbed, and sold a lot of houses and small apartment houses. In 99 percent of my deals, I have been quietly using this little known, under-utilized technique to acquire and profit from real estate all across the United States specifically in Florida, New York, Texas and California. I have to say it has got to be the easiest, cheapest and fastest method to acquire properties. This technique alone has been making me thousands of dollars per deal and keeps me in business full-time.

It all started when I had just entered New York University on only a song and a prayer, a "foreign" student on a student visa from Canada. You see I was from a poor Jamaican-Canadian family that immigrated to the United States via New York City. It was just me and my mom and we were struggling to make ends meet. I was watching TV late at nights because I couldn't sleep. I watched so many infomercials about investing in real estate and finally I decided to get involved. Carleton Sheets and Tom Vu got my attention, they "spoke" to me…. they said everything I wanted to hear that anyone could make a lot of money investing in real estate no money down. That might sound so ridiculous to you right now but at that time I would believe anything, I was broke and desperate. Anyway, a seed was sown, and it took root, that was the motivation that I needed. I dreamed about owning all kinds of properties, I saw myself owning houses and apartment buildings collecting good money and living financially free from my investments.

Then it hit me, how was I going to do this? I didn't have any money! Where would I even start? Over the next few months, I would attend every real estate seminar and investor groups I could find. It was difficult not knowing anyone and feeling like an outsider. I made no friends, no one wanted to share, in fact the people I knew wouldn't talk about how they did it, only bragged about what they did. I had some major obstacles to my dream of real estate ownership, so I quit, after all, I had no money, no credit, no income, no job, no green card, it just wasn't going to be possible for me.

It wasn't until the bill collectors came knocking…. real hard that I suddenly realized I was poorer than I thought my back was against the wall, so I decided I was going to learn by doing and test the theory of no money down real estate investing. I am so glad I did it, thanks to God, if it wasn't for prayer and persistence then I would have totally missed out on this opportunity in real estate.

I could not buy anything the conventional way – so qualifying with a job and good credit, getting a mortgage, paying down payment money and all of that was out of the question. I figured the only way I would be able to get into real estate would be to become a real estate agent. That was a bust because the only thing I learned in real estate school was about the law. So much for that! Somehow, I got into wholesaling real estate.... Well just as I feared, my buyers were trying to go around me to the owner directly, the buyers would wait me out, wait until my contract ended and then went directly to the seller, man! After I had promoted the heck out of the property, now they get to sell direct to my buyer and that left me out of the deal. Even though I had a contract on it, they would wait until I failed to close. I couldn't find a buyer and would have to bail on the deals. Then they would grab my deal close on it and make a fortune. That's when I made this change that I'm about to share with you in this book. When I became the owner, that stopped them cold, no one could go around me, because I was the owner. Looking back now I realize that it was good that they stole my deals because what was meant for my loss, God used it to make me thrive.

My first Subject-To deal was an old 3-family house that I took over in New Jersey. I just took over Subject-To the mortgage and tax liens that were on it, add to those liens the house was also in foreclosure, the owner was at his wits end. It took me about a week to "buy" this property and put it in my name. I became the owner of this 3-unit property with NO money at all! After getting into and selling this deal, I was able to pay off over $60,000 of deferred school tuition, judgments I had owed and some other stupid stuff I had gotten into after owning another business. I walked away with a cool $5,000 in my pocket after all of the bills against me were paid in full. Needless to say, I never looked back. Yes, the claims made by those crazy people on the infomercials were true after all, you *could* invest in real estate with no money down.

ALICIA A COX

@ALICIAACOX (twitter)
ALICIACOXMEDIA (YouTube)
ALICIACOXREALESTATE (Facebook)

1

Get the Deed to Beautiful Homes

While it's been said that you should get rich using other people's money, they were talking about getting loans that you have to pay back, heck that's if you can qualify to get loans. What they didn't tell you is that other people who lend you their money want it back. Please let me give you a better way to use OPM, my definition is Other People's Mortgages.

It is about taking over the owner's mortgage Subject-To the existing mortgages and liens on the property. You get on the deed and leave the existing liens in place. This real estate investing strategy is simply referred to as "Sub2" and you won't believe the beautiful homes that you could pick up and the money you could make taking over other people's mortgages.

Get the Deed! "Subject-To" the Existing Financing

How would you like to get the deed to beautiful homes in the nicest neighborhoods Subject-To their existing loans and then reselling for huge chunks of cash? We're talking $20,000 - $30,000 even $60,000 a pop? I mean you own and control these properties to do with whatever you want. We're talking the white picket fence, granite counters, nice newly built homes with the beautiful lawns. What do you think investors pay to get into these deals? I will show you how we do it, you'll see that you don't really need money to make money in real estate. You'll learn how to take over payments on other people's homes "Subject-To" the existing financing.

This is big business! This technique is being used by successful real estate investors across the USA, Canada and Europe. A friend of mind is using this technique on commercial buildings, she takes over troubled, problem properties in Los Angeles, CA. You can pretty much take over any property, anywhere. Even investors in Canada are using this technique, I spoke to several people in Toronto who are using Subject-To technique I even spoke to a dude in Germany! I have bought houses and small apartment buildings Subject-To their underlying financing in several states now and it works the same. What I'm about to show you is not only can you take over houses but other types of real estate like mobile homes, land, commercial buildings even businesses can be purchased Subject-To their existing financing.

In this book, I'll show you how this technique works and how investors are using this technique to make buckets of cash selling or renting real estate that they took overusing the very same strategies in this book. I'll show you how you can profit from any property regardless of liens even when the property is upside down and underwater! Oh, and the other side of the business is even sweeter when you cash out selling or leasing them out, you'll make cash not once but three times. If you're a wholesaler, listen up – why are you giving away your profits and leaving money on the table? Use this strategy to earn even more and profit from your hard work.

Taking over properties Subject-To the existing financing has got to be the most profitable and most creative way of getting into real estate. So, if you're looking to get into real estate investing and you don't have a lot of money, definitely look at this technique. I would suggest learning all you can about this very lucrative side of the investing business and just do it. If you are just starting in real estate with limited cash you can buy properties to flip or rent, no cash or credit needed. If you are an experienced investor and want to expand your knowledge of real estate techniques, or maybe your cash is tapped out, you too can benefit from buying real estate – no matter what your credit report says or what's in your bank account. The information here will show you how to buy any type of property, residential or commercial Subject-To the underlying, existing mortgages and liens. Keep reading my friend and you too will discover the creative side of real estate investing.

Get the Deed! "Subject-To" the Existing Financing

How Much Money Can You Make?

You can make as much or as little as you want to make, there's no glass ceiling like at the job I'm thinking you have right now.... Your goals of owning multiple properties are attainable, you can work full or part time, it's completely up to you. Work from your kitchen table or out of a corner of your bedroom. The tax benefits of owning a business and real estate are nice – you get to write off office expenses, interest and depreciation expense.

You can easily earn six figures $100,000+ per year as I did by myself because even just one deal can earn you that much. Say the average priced house in your area is $225,000 to $285,000, you purchase for $200,000 - $260,000 you sell for value or even a bit more. On average I think you could easily do $20,000 per deal and I haven't included the option fee or leasing spread that you could earn in addition. So how many of these deals do you think you could do a year? What if you could do 1 per month or even 1 every other month and you averaged $20,000 each, that's $20,000 @ 6 per year, that's $120,000 per year!

Get the Deed! "Subject-To" the Existing Financing

When you close on these deals, it will feel like you've won the lottery and you didn't have to gamble or sell weed. It feels so good to be in charge of your own destiny.

I suggest you get your fire back and start to dream again. Open your mind to the possibility of doing and having things that you stopped hoping for – like being able to quit your job and do anything you want, driving around in your Aston Martin to the mall and see the amazement of your friends and family when they finally believe you now, how about the big luxury house on the hill that you wish you could live in. Maybe it's something simpler like actually taking a good long vacation with the whole family and not having to come back to a job, or just becoming debt free, owing no one, no more debt collection calls.

This is the one business opportunity that doesn't require start up investment, office, employees, licenses or permits. This is not just a business that you even need to apply for a business license because it's an investment opportunity, not like any other business where you're selling something or a service out of your garage. You're by passing all of that…come on up higher into the investment world. You can do this! You can take this information and let it set you up for retirement and when you're well into your future you'll be glad you did something like this now. You'll be able to just sit back and live

Get the Deed! "Subject-To" the Existing Financing

on your residual investment income. You know they say that real estate is responsible for lots of millionaires, let's make one of them be you!

Get the Deed! "Subject-To" the Existing Financing

2

What is "Subject-To" Investing?

It is simply you buying a property Subject-To the underlying mortgage loans and liens. You take over someone else's mortgage payments without you having to get a new loan. You get title to the property but you leave the seller's name on the loan with the existing loan staying in place. You take over properties with no formal assumptions. The seller deeds you the property, you become the new owner, the loan stays in the seller's name and you take over the payments.

Buying subject also means that all of the mortgages, the terms of the note like the interest rate and terms stays the same and you will just step into the seller's shoes and keep making the payments as agreed. This is not a formal loan assumption, where you apply for and qualify to assume a loan no, you are not assuming anything neither are you liable.

Get the Deed! "Subject-To" the Existing Financing

It sounds complicated but I promise you it is not. Some people even think it's illegal but actually Subject-To is legit. As a matter of fact, look at the Closing Disclosure on page 3, in the middle of the page, on line 3 of both the buyer's side and the seller's side, "Existing Loans(s) Assumed or Taken Subject-To"

You can take over nice homes in nice areas, believe it or not these are easiest. The same can be done with Junkers, mobile homes, apartment houses, commercial property, as long as you have this knowledge, you can get the deed! Here are some benefits, when you buy properties subject-to the existing mortgages: We'll discuss the opportunities that exists just because you're on title. We'll also discuss situations where the seller pays you for taking the deed. Here are some advantages of buying Subject-To:

1. There's absolutely no qualifying
2. No loan fees – no borrowing
3. Close super fast
4. Buy as many homes as you want without capping out.
5. Buy homes with little to no equity
6. You're helping by preventing a foreclosure
7. Lender minimizes loss
8. You control and make all decisions

Get the Deed! "Subject-To" the Existing Financing

9. You get the tax benefits
10. Profit from appreciation
11. Profit from built in equity
12. Profit from monthly cash flow

Let's take a deeper dive into the advantages:

There is absolutely no qualifying. No new loan means no qualifying for any mortgage or from anybody. In fact, no one is qualifying you, the seller does not qualify you because you are not asking the seller to finance you, you are just taking over his loan. The exception here is if the seller does not have a mortgage and they own free and clear, then they could choose to give seller-financing in this case it would be different and not a subject-to deal.

No loan fees since you're not borrowing. You won't have to get a new mortgage to buy the property, which makes these deals easy and quick to get into. You eliminate lender fees and any new cost of borrowing. The only exception would be the escrow and title costs when using a title and escrow company.

You can close fast. Because you can close fast, you'll be able to solve the sellers' problems quickly and this is what is required most of the time. The seller has financial problems and would like to see it go away as quickly as possible.

You can buy as many as you want. You are not limited to the amount you can buy like when you finance properties. When they are financed, lenders limit the amount of money they will lend and label you high risk. This stops you from accumulating more or forces you to put a blanket loan on multiple properties.

Unique strategy you can buy houses with little or no equity. It is possible to take over property that is over-leveraged or upside down and still make money. Keep reading, I'll explain this later.

You're helping people, rescuing them from foreclosure. You have an important role in your community because you keep the ball rolling. Instead of going into foreclosure, you can help people to "save face" and move on while you prevent a bank from foreclosing on a homeowner.

You're helping the lender also because you help minimize a potential loss. There are more than one ways that a lender could lose if they foreclose. For one thing, it stops them from lending more when they have non-performing assets on their books, second, it costs money to foreclose. They have to pay lawyers, court fees, trustee services and other expenses to take back a property. Thirdly, it's not a politically correct thing to do right now. Fourthly, who knows what kind of damages they will have to deal with after they kick out the homeowner/borrower, there may be city code violations to deal with, squatters and who knows if they'll be able to recover the loan from re-selling or if they would be able to re-sell.

You control the property and make all the decisions. After you take over and everything is in your name, you have full ownership. Even though it will not be your name on the loan documents, you have the deed to the property. This means you can rent it, sell it, keep it, put more financing on it, refinance it, all the things a homeowner can do.

You get all the tax benefits. If not for any other reason, this should perk you up. In the US, it's like we literally get paid to own real estate. It's so much fun to write off the mortgage interest and depreciation at tax time. It pays to take over real estate and keep it.

You will profit from the appreciation. Buying and holding is how you build wealth. You build wealth not only when you collect rent on your properties but also as time goes by they are appreciating in value.

As you pay down the mortgage you profit from the equity. By the time you get to the homeowner, he may have paid years of mortgage interest on the property. Did you know that most of the monthly payment is mostly interest at the beginning of the loan? So when you take over, more of the principal would be paid down in your monthly payments, this means, the house is being paid down faster the longer you pay on that loan. So why pay it off?

You will collect monthly cash flow. Another way you make money is when you collect more than you pay out, this is called the spread. This is spendable cash, this amount for me is usually $200-$500 per house, per month.

The idea of Subject-To investing has many benefits for everyone; the investor, the seller and the lender. Subject-To benefits the investor because there is low dollar entry to the deal and multiple profit potential. It benefits the seller because he gets to walk away from debt problems and provides immediate debt relief. It benefits the lender because it mitigates his losses and prevents a foreclosure. Subject-To may not be the only answer to all situations but it can provide a win-win-win opportunity to all parties which makes it a wonderful technique.

Why Would a Seller Sell Subject-To?

The thing is they are motivated by something, that's why the ones you approach must be motivated. If they are just sitting at home wondering what they can get for the house and don't have an urgency to move, then they are only motivated by price and not motivated enough to agree on terms. Anyone can become a motivated seller at any time. All it takes is something in life to happen and suddenly everything changes. The truly motivated seller has given up on his property and is seeking a way to get out. He is willing to lose everything and just walk away whether or not they get anything for their property. When you think of the reasons why someone could become motivated to sell then you won't think it's so ridiculous or unbelievable. It's powerful. It's like the man who would risk everything to be with the woman he loves or the woman who would walk away with nothing just to get away from someone or something. These are some of the circumstances that create urgency and need:

Problem #1 Relocation

Seller is relocating because of a job transfer, they are retiring and moving back down south or to be closer to family. Also along these same lines a seller may be moving into an assisted type living facility and wants to unload property now. There's an urgent need and they can't wait, the home has been on the market for some time but no takers. While this house sits on the market it stops seller from leaving and moving on. Time is the most important factor here, not money, so if you can buy now, they'll be able to move on instead of lingering.

Problem #2 Family Matters

Seller has personal problems and might be going through a divorce, illness, aging, empty nester. How would you deal with having your income decreased but can't get the expenses lowered to match? These sellers need their problem solved now so that they can move on and start over.

Problem #3 Financial Distress

The biggest reason I see is for financial distress. The seller has bought another property and has moved away and is now having hardship because he's making two mortgage payments. Or what if the seller lost their job or got downsized? Can you see how this would affect his ability to pay his mortgage? Often it is some combination of the above that causes seller to sink deep into financial distress. Now they want to just stop making payments and just walk away. They need debt relief immediately. My niche of choice was with the seller who was in financial distress, they are usually in foreclosure,

Problem #4 Property Distress

There is little or no equity left in the house or they owe much more than the property is worth, they are underwater. How are they going to sell a house like this without a short sale? You can offer them this solution.

Get the Deed! "Subject-To" the Existing Financing

3

The "Subject-To" Secret

The secret to making the most money with this technique is by understanding some key points.

Secret #1 Ownership & Debt.

There is a difference between ownership and debt, that is who's on the title and who is on the mortgage. Those two are not necessarily the same persons. It is possible as you will see, to have one party be on the ownership and title and the other party on the security instrument alone, that is the mortgage. The most important thing to remember about Subject-To investing is the difference between debt and title. Once you've grasped the mechanics of this type of transaction it will be easy to master this technique. Essentially when you take over a mortgage, you are buying Subject-To the terms and agreements of the existing loans, liens. The seller is transferring title to the property to you and you are preserving and keeping the original terms of the underlying loan.

The seller is in effect providing seller financing, he signs the title over and title changes hands but the seller will still have formal liability for the loan in place.

Secret #2 You're a Problem Solver

Understand who you are in the transaction. Do not walk up to the seller with the idea of stealing their house, you are a problem solver and you're there to offer help, not to take it away from them and kick them out of their house. The kind of problem solver you are is the one that would help buy groceries if needed, the kind that would refer them to an attorney and back off if necessary. No two deals are alike, you never know what you'll find but you've got basically one solution, and that's debt relief.

Secret #3 Offer a Solution

You need to listen and offer a win-win **solution.** So many times I've won the seller over simply by listening and seeking to understand him/her without judgment. Many times before I even get to the house the seller had already decided just from speaking with me over the phone that they're prepared to work with me because they trust me. Trust goes a long way. Limits exists in the mind, not in the real world. You can make this happen in 30 days or less.

Secret #4 Got Problems?

A motivated seller is the one with problems, you get to solve the problems and that's when you make money. Problems equal money if you can offer the right solutions. You might be worried that this is taking advantage of people with problems, let me tell you that it's being in the right place at the right time, offering the right solution, nothing wrong with selling the prescription. I look at the distress seller as the custodian to the property that I want to buy and if I give him what he wants, he'll give me what I want.

Secret #5 Why it Works

It works because you understand the motivation behind each party. The seller needs debt relief because of problems, the lender just wants their payments and nobody wants a foreclosure. It's a WIN-WIN-WIN situation because you get to buy the house without a mortgage. It's a good arrangement because everybody wins.

4

How to Find Motivated Sellers

The main idea is to find people with real estate who are in distress, a/k/a real people with real problems. First, let me address one important point about finding the motivated seller, you could be the answer to someone's prayers. You become a problem solver and that's why they need you. So focus on finding the distressed seller not on finding properties.

Subject-to transactions are legit. And the success of Subject-To transactions depends on you and finding an agreeable seller. Notice I said agreeable not desperate. Sometimes they are one in the same other times they are not. When you come upon the resistant, skeptic it simply means that they just aren't motivated enough, often, it's simply because they don't understand and need more information. Don't take it personally and don't try to coerce them, let them find their way to you, that's going to be a better deal. Sometimes these come around, yes when the going gets rough and things hit the fan…they'll come around.

The first thing in your playbook is to find Subject-To deals and keep 'em coming. To do this well, you will use a mixture, a recipe that will become yours. Start by placing small ads locally both online and in small newspapers. Remember, the urgent seller is the owner with a big need to get rid of his or her property and quickly. They cannot wait for a conventional sale but there are special circumstances that makes that situation urgent. To understand your seller, think about the dynamics of the situation that your potential seller may be going through. Time, money, emotions, health are running out and the longer it takes for them to solve the problem, the more receptive to alternative options they will be. This is the ideal situation for an investor to offer Subject-To terms.

Getting Motivated Sellers to Call You

One of the best ways we get motivated sellers to call you is to advertise where they advertise, the For Sale By Owner, (FSBO). When you get them to call you, you're in control and get to ask all the questions. It's a different scenario when they call you, it identifies them as the one needing your help and so they've called you for a service. They're in effect, raising their hand and they are coming knocking on your door for help. The dynamics of the negotiation and your posture is significantly different when the sellers call us. We are more in the position to control the conversation and to ask questions and extract information. I find that I can get more information from a seller and obtain answers to questions that I couldn't get when I'm the one calling them on their advertising.

Use online sources like Craigslist, FaceBook, InstaGram and local free newspapers (the kind you find thrown on your lawn or walking over in your driveway). These free papers work well and they are inexpensive to advertise in. You'll be advertising that you buy houses and take over payments. Keep your advertising simple, you don't need 100 calls a day, you only need targeted, motivated sellers with an urgent need to call you.

Target Market: So what does the property look like? I say property because it may not be a house that you take over. My first Sub2 was a multi-unit apartment building. Houses however, are plentiful in the market and more people need them, there's a stronger demand for homes than commercial property. So I would advise searching for houses first.

Get the Deed! "Subject-To" the Existing Financing

The house that you're looking for is well kept, the lawn is watered and it may be vacant. You won't find these houses on the foreclosure list and the seller may not be behind on payments. You will find that the seller is actively selling the house on Craigslist or FSBO websites including Zillow. Their ads are the long flowing ads that lets you know everything about everything that's been done and the nice kitchen, etc.

The other kind of house you're looking for is the nice house with the dead lawn. It could be vacant and may or may not have the power on. This happens when people are in financial problems, one of the first things to go is the lawn. In either case, the house you're looking for is in a newer community, built 1-5 years ago by one of the tract home builders like KB Homes, D.R. Horton, Lennar and the like. These sellers bought new at top price. There is no equity, in fact they may be upside down and there-in lies the problem. They cannot really sell because they owe more than the market value of the house. If they were to list with a realtor, they would have to sell it at market and come to closing with the difference. For instance, they owe $225,000 but they can't get more than $200,000 for it, so they're $25,000 short. That would cause them to have to come out of pocket $25,000 in order to pay off the existing mortgage. Most people are not going to do that and to also pay a real estate commission. Most realtors will list the house and

Get the Deed! "Subject-To" the Existing Financing

hope the lender will accept a short sale but the seller might not even qualify for a short sale, now what?

I can't talk about short sale without saying this first, they don't look good on your credit report and that's why some sellers will be against it. What about the seller who cannot get a short sale even if they wanted one? These sellers are non-owner occupants, investors or people who just don't fit the parameters of those who would qualify. A short sale assumes that the owner is insolvent, so if someone had to relocate because of a job promotion let's say, should he lie and say, he lost his job and wants to sell his house short? Absolutely not! and this is my point, some won't even qualify for a short sale, some won't want one, yet they are upside down and have negative equity. This type of seller needs you.

Here are some of the top methods I have used to get sellers to call me. "We Buy Houses" always works, it's vague and simple and it leaves the door open to all kinds of offers. Be prepared for all kinds of calls, from realtors, from wholesalers and from other real estate investors or just curious people. Depending on your area and what you come up with, you will get calls from sellers with Junkers as well as homes needing no repairs. All are good potential for an opportunity, however not all opportunities will be right for you. If you're more interested in something move in ready like me and don't want to have to fix anything, then look for the newer homes in suburbia and go to them using direct mail.

WE BUY HOUSES

Keep it simple, works well. I do not advocate advertising for "Cash for your home" because if somebody is motivated by cash they will call, however that's not what you're offering. That's a little deceptive, unless you have a line of credit where you can offer cash on the spot. These messages could be used on yard signs, flyers, ads, post cards and door hangers.

Handling Incoming Calls. Depending on your area, you will get calls, people will call wanting to know what it's about and if you can buy their house. This is your opportunity to find out as much as you can about their motivation and information about the house. Steer the conversation to lead to a visit so that you can meet them and inspect the property. For heaven's sake, get the address right. Next, you will jump on the internet and just pop the address onto Google. What you're looking for is anything that will pop up with that address, pictures, listings on Zillow, directions, etc. Then go over the Property Information Worksheet, a/k/a Subject-To Deal Sheet and copy all that information onto your deal sheet. There in front of you on one page is all the info you'll need to make your decisions. Also this form will serve as a point of reference for when you prepare your Subject-To documents. It's also a great conversation starter, the form will also help you to stay on topic by asking the right questions during the phone call with the seller. Visit our website to download a free copy.

Get the Deed! "Subject-To" the Existing Financing

5

How to Get the Deed

Why would anyone agree to sign over their property Subject-To their mortgage? This is one of the biggest questions I get when I tell people what I do. They cannot comprehend how this could be that someone would sell their house Subject-To the mortgage, signing over the deed to me and still be liable for the mortgage. That's because they don't understand the degree of motivation someone else might have that is forcing the issue and the degree of stress the seller might have.

As I've said before, everyone has their own stress level and what stresses you out and messes you up may not bother me because not everyone is on the same level of stress and is not the same for everyone. That's why we target people in certain situations and go directly to the potential seller and have them call us.

Benefit to the seller. You are a one stop shop, you help them to deal with problems and special circumstances like, seller needs cash, property needs rehab, property has no equity, seller hasn't made any payments for a while and is behind in payments, seller wants to stay, there are two mortgages, liens, there is a Notice of Default, a Notice Of Sale is pending, seller filed for bankruptcy, the taxes and insurance are past due, there are code violations on property, the mortgage is an adjustable rate mortgage, there are prepayment penalties if they sell or refinance, association dues and fees are overdue. All of these problems you can solve.

Gather the Data. The first thing I do is get out my Subject-To Deal Sheet and plug in the numbers, I'm getting all my information from title company, online places like Zillow, Redfin, and most importantly that county's recorders' office or the appraisers office, which ever one has owner and property information. Then I'll use my worksheet and come up with a buy price. I detail all of this in my course, too long for this book. Once I have my buy price, I go to talk to the seller and to look at the property.

Get the Deed! "Subject-To" the Existing Financing

The Visit. At the property, I'm talking to the owner and establishing rapport while I'm having a look around. By the end of my visit, I know all about the house and the owner. Before I leave the home, I'm letting them know whether or not I'm interested and if I'll be making an offer. Back at my home office, I prepare an LOI or a Purchase Agreement with my subject-to clauses. Then I go back to the seller and present my offer.

Negotiating with the Seller. I use a worksheet when I'm negotiating the purchase. A key component to negotiating the subject-to deal is to let it be all about them and their situation. Stress how it will solve their problem and how quickly they'll be able to sell and without a Realtor® commission. The fun part for them is when you tell them when you'll be taking over their mortgage payments. It's not uncommon to take over payments within a 60-90-day period after closing, it depends on the needs of the seller and what you negotiate.

The Purchase Agreement

Up to this point we've been talking about who would sign over the deed, finding the motivated seller and gathering the data. As you can imagine, you need to put it under contract. I know, you thought you could just grab the deed while you were over there. Actually, you could but more than likely you need more than this to convince the seller to give up the deed. Your approach should be honest, straight forward and formal. You will be making an offer my friend. For this offer we use a Purchase Contract.

The purchase agreement is important because it governs your transaction. I try to use a purchase form that is common to the local area and simply ad my subject-to language and disclosures. In California it's the CAR form or the First Tuesday forms, but you know we investors have got to have our own. I have an investor friendly one that I put in the Get the Deed "Subject-To" The Existing Mortgage course. It has specific Subject-To language that is only for this type of deal.

Basically, you'll make your offer on a contract form, spelling out the purchase price and include closing instructions, just like a regular sale, the only difference are the terms. The terms are not cash but Subject-To the existing, underlying liens and loans and I include my subject-to clauses in my contract. You'll even include an earnest money deposit in order to create a bona-fide purchase agreement. Relax, it will be for a nominal amount and that check stays with you until you're ready to close. Then you create disclosures about the transactions that explains the subject-to transaction that your seller is agreeing to. It's all in the open and you will provide your seller with copies of what they sign.

Got Deed?

While it is possible to just get a deed signed over without paperwork or purchase agreements, I would not recommend it. You want a real sale not just a deed. Yes, I'll admit there was a time when I would meet the desperate seller somewhere in the driveway signing papers on top of the hood of the car and shaking hands through the window… Yes, it was easy but there could be problems when you go to resell after if you didn't get all of the selling paperwork signed. It's beneficial to have power of attorney signed and a HUD-1 prepared as well, more in the course. I know an investor in New York that was just goes around buying deeds. He was very aggressively collecting deeds willy-nilly, paying off the owners to leave and then banks the deeds. That was before he contacted me, then I set him straight with forms and a system. He had his attorney call me and we worked out every detail, now he's a happy subject-to investor with a portfolio of houses.

Get the Deed! "Subject-To" the Existing Financing

The Subject-To Deal Sheet

As you start receiving calls and fielding questions, you will need someplace to collect your data. This place is what I call a "Subject-To Deal Sheet." You will collect information on the property and on the owner. Everything from how many people are on title, if it's listed or not, how many beds, bath, tax info, market value, default status and mortgage information. It is a one-page document that helps you figure out buy price and what exit strategy to use. I'll be happy to send this form to you free. I'll have it available at my course site. See the back of this book for links.

This same thing can be accomplished electronically via a spreadsheet, however, this form can be printed or used on your iPad. I used to give myself a challenge to see how many of these forms I can collect. Then I would file them my month in a binder, then when someone calls me back, I have it handy and I know everything I need to talk sensibly to the seller. It's simple and it's easy.

So, you will collect all the data on your deal sheet which will become your blueprint for the rest of the process. You will know your buy price, sell price and the best exit strategy to take. This is the sheet that you could take to investors like me to partner with you or get help on.

6

The Art of Closing the Deal

After you've presented the offer and the seller signs your Purchase Agreement, it's time to move to closing the deal. Closing Subject-To deals are informal and you want to make it as easy going and stress free for the seller as possible. That's the key to getting and keeping a cooperative seller. No matter where or what means you use, the kitchen table, on top of the hood of your car or escrow/title company you will prepare your paperwork and close within the specified time stress free and easy.

It is recommended that you get title and possession together at the closing table immediately after closing, otherwise we could have other issues. So, after the seller signs the paperwork you should get the keys and then change the locks, title and possession. However, it is best to do as agreed, if you agreed to leave the seller in there, let's say for another month, then that's what you should do. As for me, I would not agree to close the deal unless I am going to receive both title and possession at closing. Don't risk them staying longer than agreed or worst, changing their minds…that could cause too many problems. So my advice would be to keep it simple, do not alleviate the pain until you get what you want, that's the deed and the keys.

A key component to closing your subject-to deal is arranging when you'll take over the mortgage payments, when you'll start making payments on the seller's mortgage. This is an agreement you make not something written in stone anywhere. Although the seller would like to see the problems go away today, the changing of when you take over the sellers' mortgage payment needs to benefit you as well as the seller.

So, you calculate your profit before you even see the property by finding true market value and a buy price then you will verify this information once you've seen the property and get seller's mortgage information. Once you've examined the seller's interest rate and mortgage balance, you can figure your profit. You will get the profit at the exit strategy.

THE Close. By the time you're sitting around the kitchen table or at a table at Starbucks, you would have already prepared the paperwork. I go over all of this in the Get the Deed Subject-To online course and I provide the forms for this process.

Get the Deed! "Subject-To" the Existing Financing

You can use a title company/escrow company to close or an attorney, you should use whatever is customary in your area. In Los Angeles, we use escrow companies to close, in Florida we use title companies, in New Jersey we use attorneys. A word of caution when using these, I've found that they like to take over your deal and act like you don't know anything. I do not like this, so I attempt to always control my deal and only involve them when I'm ready to close. I've found an even better way is to only use them to pull title (not absolutely necessary) and most of the time I don't use them at all. I just use a notary, the kind that knows how to sign loans (signing notary) and the kitchen table.

Recap, calculate your profit before you buy. Obtain the following information from the mortgage statement: mortgage balance, note payment, interest rate. Get the market value from public sources like Zillow, Redfin, Realtor® websites. Verify this information by contacting the sellers' lender.

Get the Deed! "Subject-To" the Existing Financing

What to Do After You Take Over Title

Got the Deed – Now What? Oh snap! What just happened here? You got the deed Yo!

After the closing is done, your work begins. The homeowner insurance, mortgage, taxes all have to be amended, people have to be notified. You can do all of this online. These steps must be followed immediately after closing takes place. The entire system is too lengthy for this book, but you can get this information by getting the full course.

Title & Ownership. Every property has an owner, he that controls, makes decisions to sell, rent, incur expense, repair build upon etc. The legal entity that holds title to a property could be natural persons, corporations/limited liability companies or trusts. As title is conveyed to another, all the rights and decision goes to the new owner and that right is conveyed via a deed.

When title is transferred several things happen:

- A New Deed is prepared in the name of the new owner
- The owner has to sign over, convey the title by signing the deed to the receiving party.
- The New Deed is filed and recorded at the county recorder's office for the world to see.

Get the Deed! "Subject-To" the Existing Financing

Always take title in a trust, some investors just take title in their LLC which is fine, but it raises the red flag of title transfer. I explain this more in my free videos on YouTube.

Get the Deed! "Subject-To" the Existing Financing

7

The Exit Strategy

Finding buyers isn't difficult at all. Selling is the fun part because that's when you'll see the money you've worked so hard for. You'll be offering a much needed, valued product, a good home to live in that they don't have to qualify for. Think about the people who will most likely be leasing from you. They maybe just getting out of foreclosure or a bankruptcy.

After having a house, it's going to be tough squeezing you, your stuff, the two kids, the dog and puss into an apartment again. Back then it was just himself and his wife, now he's got a family and all that stuff in the garage. This person really needs a home like yours to put up them and their family. The thing is their credit is not so good right now due to some problems….

When I qualify my buyers, I don't focus that much on the credit, and I don't judge…. only to the point of qualifying them eventually, say in 1-2 years. This works out just fine since I'll need that time anyway to make sure the property appraises for a higher amount than what it was when I took it over.

It's best to use a loan officer to prequalify your buyers, this way he or she will stay with your buyers and help them to qualify so that there will be a loan for them at the end of the lease term.

What happens if the buyers don't qualify or they are not ready by the end of the term? Then I renew the lease with the option and increase the lease amount and the price of the property also goes up, not by much but say an extra $10,000. Okay, now let's move into your exit and back end strategy.

Your exit strategies could be:

Leasing – You could just do a straight rental and rent forever.

Selling – You could just turn around a sell quick to an end buyer.

Lease with Option – My favorite exit strategy because you're helping someone who might have problems buying immediately so you're giving them a chance to own.

Deciding exit strategy. It really depends on what you've got, because you can only sell what you've got. For example, if you acquired the property with no equity then it wouldn't make sense to turn around and sell right away. This means you'll have

Get the Deed! "Subject-To" the Existing Financing

to *Sell High* and *Sell Long*, meaning sell it in 2-3 years instead of now or a year from now. Likewise, if you acquired the property and you used my bank negotiation strategy to create equity and reduce the principal balance, then you could afford to *Sell Low*, meaning you can "wholetail" or sell just below full value and make a quick profit without touching or repairing the property.

Fact is, there are buyers everywhere who will be waiting in line to get into your houses. In fact, I have more buyers than I have houses for. I have a small business in Florida who will pay me top dollar to house their employees, I have people relocating to Los Angeles who need a home, they call me up begging me to find them a house that they can rent-to-own and the list goes on and on. If you didn't already guess, you can do business in all the states you want, so if it's not working for you where you are, then take it somewhere else. In fact, I like to take the show on the road and even though I'm living in Los Angeles, I'm able to put under contract and take over properties in New York, Texas and Florida. How would you like to do that?

Get the Deed! "Subject-To" the Existing Financing

Filling Your Homes Super-Fast

Advertising for buyers continuously is the way you keep your homes leased. The best way to start this business is to find your buyer first. Advertise for your buyer first so that you can see who's in your market and what they want. I've always liked the rent to own concept. In most cities it's a popular way to sell used cars, furniture and even appliances. By far the best rent to own application is in real estate which we call the lease/option deal. This is my favorite part of the transaction when I get to put a deserving family into my homes. When you offer a rent to own home, you are offering a great product that people will pay premium rent for the opportunity. If you keep this in mind it will help you to structure your deals going in.

RENT TO OWN – NO BANK QUALIFYING

Beautiful 3 bedroom/ 2 bath home, close to all, rent with option to buy.

1 or 2 years. Credit problems OK, your job is your credit.

Let's make a deal. Call (xxx) xxx-xxxx

Get the Deed! "Subject-To" the Existing Financing

You get paid three ways:

- Get paid by a non-refundable deposit called an option fee. This fee is a consideration that the buyer pays you to option your home.
- Get paid on the spread between the mortgage payment and the money you receive monthly from your buyer who is also leasing from you.
- Get paid from the profit you make at the end of the transaction, when the buyer exercises his option to buy and gets a mortgage and cashes you out. It's the difference between what you paid and the price at which you sell the house.
- Get paid from the tax deduction from depreciation, property expense deductions and mortgage interest deductions.

Processing Your Tenant-Buyers. Do it just like a management company because that's what you are now. If you don't like this part of the business, you can hire a property manager or just use a Realtor® to lease up the home.

Get the Deed! "Subject-To" the Existing Financing

8

Creative Techniques to Building Wealth

Let me talk to you about building massive wealth super-fast. It's true that you build wealth from buying and holding but did you know that you could build wealth even faster by providing short term rentals. The market is quite large and where you fit in depends on the properties you take over. For instance, you could focus on downtown properties like really nice condos in the sky. You could hold these properties and rent out like corporate rentals, like a hotel. You provide the linens, pots and pans, knives and forks, furnishings, everything except the food. Your guests are businesspeople who need long term stay for a month or more. These tenants pay top dollar for the privilege of renting something that is like a hotel but more like a home away from home.

Get the Deed! "Subject-To" the Existing Financing

There are all sorts of opportunities here, homes for the aged, homes for students, homes for special needs people and so on. Just think of the many uses or exit strategies you can use, like helping others by renting short term like a group home. You'll never have to "qualify" for a loan to purchase real estate again, at least if you don't want to.

Airbnb and sites like it are very exciting opportunities are worth checking out. Once you acquire the property, you just hold it as a vacation rental for as long as you want. There are people all over Los Angeles including rich areas like Beverly Hills who are making a killing doing this. From regular everyday apartment to the executive style villa, the possibilities are endless. I know a guy who is doing Airbnb on his studio apartment in Los Angeles and he doesn't even own the place, he's renting it. The dude clears about $3,000-$4,000 per month! If only he knew how to take over properties Subject-To, he would be crushing it even more.

Check out for yourself how this works, sign up for an account at Airbnb and research people and places in your own areas. For top dollar from out-of-town guests, you should get properties in the town areas that are close to places like the ball stadium, the airport or business centers, just think of the possibilities.

Get the Deed! "Subject-To" the Existing Financing

Creating Unlimited Cash Flow

If you've read this far it means that you are really interested in buying real estate Subject-To and I want to reward you for your time. So here is some real stuff…

I've showed you how you can take over nice homes in nice areas, I've showed you where they are and who owns them. In the previous examples, you are dealing with FSBOs who really need to sell, and they know it. How about those who are desperate and have to sell? You see the truth is you can take over anything, anywhere in any condition and the real down in the trenches 411 is that a lot of money is in helping the desperate owner. Notice I switched from the word "Seller"? Keep reading.

What most successful real estate investor buying and selling houses won't tell you is how they buy whatever they have. They're not out there getting mortgages and putting down huge down payments. No! They're buying Subject-To and then fixing and selling, they're buying Subject-To and then "whole tailing" (not a typo) it means selling above wholesale and below retail to someone else who just wants a good deal.

Get the Deed! "Subject-To" the Existing Financing

Investors are buying pre-foreclosures, by approaching people in foreclosure and taking the deed Subject-To the foreclosure, making up the back payments and bringing the loan current. They'll go as far as paying the homeowner to move, then take over the home and renting it out. Then they'll do this over and over until they have lots of these houses. If you can take over deeds and mortgage payments with no qualifying, how many of these homes can you buy? The answer is all of them.

Buying houses out of foreclosure could be the ticket you're looking for. It's an aggressive business, a lot of people are doing it but not everybody is good at it. You have to have the stomach or should I say the heart for it. Personally, I love it! This is where I "live" and can I tell you a secret? I never use any money doing these deals and I make a minimum of $20K per deal, in fact, if I'm not making at least $20K on the deal, I'm not doing it…too small, throw that one back.

Multiple Ways of Income. Let me show you some ways they are doing it.

Buy Sub2, Fix & Sell. Investors are employing apprentices called "bird dogs" and they're paying them to find Junkers and then negotiate a JV (joint venture) with the seller, taking the deed or getting on the seller's deed. They then get store card like Home Depot and Lowes, credit all the materials and compete the rehab. Then they refinance the seller off the deed or if they took the deed, refinance and payoff the seller and take the profit. They like to refi instead of selling because the cash is tax free, no tax on loans. Then they sell the property and do it again.

Buy Pre-Foreclosures before bank takes it over. Investors approach indebted homeowner who is struggling with his bank. Takes the deed and then negotiates the lien with the bank, receives a short sale and then "wholetails" the property. Buy pre-foreclosures forget foreclosures.

Sub2 Pre-Foreclosure – Sale Date. Investor approaches borrowers in default in the Sheriff Sale or Notice of Sale status. Note this is the last stage of the foreclosure before the bank takes the property. Since time is of an essence, the homeowner has to act fast and usually at this stage they've either given up and left the home vacant or are ready to. At this point anything you offer them is "found money" so they are quick to co-operate. Investor makes a few interesting moves to slow down the bank and delays the foreclosure sale long enough to fix the problem. Through negotiations and delay tactics investor makes a lot of money for his efforts.

Sub2 Pre-Foreclosure – Live Free. Investor obtains the deed Subject-To the mortgage loan in default and moves into the home. Investor uses delay tactics to prevent the bank from foreclosing and lives payment free until he is ready to negotiate a short sale or loan modification. If the bank forecloses and the investor loses, he might be able to get cash for keys or negotiate with the new buyer that purchased the home at the foreclosure sale. Investor could have gone to the auction and purchased the property as well.

Sub2 Pre-Foreclosure – Save the Sale. Investor obtains the deed and obtains a buyer then goes to the auction and purchases the house after foreclosure. Takes the deed back to the anxious buyer and saves the sale. Works really well on higher end properties where the buyer has obtained his mortgage and is ready to buy but the bank forecloses. Instead of the Realtor® losing the sale he could have an investor go to auction purchasing the property and re-selling to buyer for a profit.

There's some more crazy stuff but they're too crazy to mention, but the real stuff I mention works. You're high on the food chain and you could eat for days. The challenge is what to do with all that money.

Buying subject-to gives you the option of exit strategies, you get the most opportunities to set up your income to receive multiple properties in different kinds of ways and with very little everyday effort. You can be as involved as you want to be deferring some of the roles to outside companies. Eventually

Get the Deed! "Subject-To" the Existing Financing

what you could achieve is passive monthly income that surpasses your current income that you make per year. Another benefit to doing this business is the benefit you get from appreciation, if you had the properties. This is truly passive income, and you get to deduct the expenses and depreciation on your taxes.

Get the Deed! "Subject-To" the Existing Financing

Get the Deed! "Subject-To" the Existing Financing

9

The Due on Sale Clause

Every loan these days will have a clause that says if the borrower decides to sell then the lenders' loan will be due and payable upon transfer of the property. The "due on sale" clause says that upon a sale, the lender has the right to call the entire loan balance due and payable. This clause is there to protect the lender and not really the seller. So, what happens when we take deeds Subject-To? The lender can call the loan due; do they call the loan? Usually not. I've never seen that happen; it only happens when somebody doesn't make the loan payments that's when the lender tries to foreclose.

The lender is more concerned with making a profit. They make a profit from the spread between principal and interest. So, if their loan was at a higher interest rate than current market rate, they would not want to cancel the loan just to have it refinanced at a lower rate, this wouldn't be a good move for them. Actually, they are punished by the Federal Government because that loan has become a non-performing note which stops them from lending that much more. So, calling a loan or foreclosing on a mortgage is bad business, it's bad for business.

My system allows for this and allows you to take over deeds without triggering the due on sale clause. It's not bullet-proof but it works like a charm. I accomplish this by the use of a trust.

There really isn't anything to really worry about, it's not something signed into law by a body of the United States government, there isn't a due on sale jail or even a fine for breaking the due on sale clause. The only punishment is that the lender *could* call the loan due. In 100% of my deals, I have never had a loan called due because I purchased via Subject-To.

Working with The Lender

Suppose you found a property that was in foreclosure, the seller has not been paying his mortgage for about a year and the lender is offering the borrower help. You can help out by having the seller sign an Authorization to Release Loan

Get the Deed! "Subject-To" the Existing Financing

Information allowing you to speak with his lender about his loan. You call the bank and talk to the loan reps verifying and asking for information. You'll want to work with the lender to do a loan modification or a short sale. Sometimes the property is so far upside down and well into the foreclosure process that the smartest thing to do is a short sale. Then you will already have your exit strategy cut out for you. With a short sale, you seek to short the mortgage so much as to allow for a below market purchase price. Here you'll have to be ready with your exit strategy with your own mortgage to take it out of the foreclosure.

But we're talking about not having to qualify to get any mortgages, right? fear not, you can still negotiate your short sale and then turn around and sell to another buyer. The profit is in the difference between your purchase price from the bank and your sales price to your buyer.

Negotiating Liens with Lien Holders

When we take over properties subject-to sometimes there are more than one loans on the property and sometimes there are other liens that are not mortgage loans. I've seen and worked

Get the Deed! "Subject-To" the Existing Financing

with IRS liens, judgments, contractor mechanic liens and tax liens. These are more common with higher end properties and commercial properties. Again, they are not as difficult to deal with they only look intimidating.

I once took over a Junker that was in foreclosure in a city in South Florida. The owner signed over the deed to me and took off, I mean exit, stage right.... gone!. There were tax liens, and contractor liens in addition to the mortgage that were in default. The city had also placed a lien on the property for a code violation for a ridiculous amount of money. It's no wonder why the seller couldn't sell the house, it was a Junker, add to that the liens turned out to be way more than the house was worth. The house was worth maybe $85K as is with an after repaired value of around $165K, more if I was willing to add square footage. The seller had no way of fixing the problems, he was broke, and his wife took the kids and left him. He would have to sell for around $250K to get rid of all the problems he had, so by the time I got to him he was ready to run. Not even the rehabbers wanted it because they didn't know what to do with it all those crazy liens, they looked intimidating.

So, I took the deed and negotiated the liens myself with each lien holder. The bank discounted because they were afraid of dealing with the city's code violation and the IRS. If they'd foreclose, they would have to pay out more than they could sell

Get the Deed! "Subject-To" the Existing Financing

the house for, so they let me have it at a deep discount. I got the IRS to lift their lien entirely. I fixed the fence problem and stump grounded the dead tree that the city had a problem with. The city gave me a whopping $34,000 discount. The lien was for $35K, I got it down to...wait for it...a mere $235! Whaat?!! That was one of the happiest days of my life, I felt so good, like I'm a badass cause I kicked some ass up in here! I simply presented myself as the new owner and showed my receipts for the work that I had done, and the city loved it. The only problem was the tax lien, the company that had bought the tax liens wouldn't budge, so I had to pay them off in full. I made more money from that stinky old, run down house than I had from the homes that had only one mortgage and no liens. There is money in those liens if you take the time to negotiate them.

Get the Deed! "Subject-To" the Existing Financing

10

Working with Sellers in Foreclosure

One of my favorite types of deals to get into is the property with little or no equity, in fact it's nicer when they are way over-leveraged. I'm talking 100% negative equity. In fact, one of my latest deal that I did was on a higher end property that lost its value during the great recession of 2008. They purchased the home pre-recession for 695,000 a good then but now as of this writing the value is only about $325,000 barely and they now owed $985,000, (foreclosure fees, back taxes, etc....).

Owner contacted me after she received a Notice of Sale. She hadn't paid her mortgage for over 8 years! and now the bank came knocking with a big fat Notice of Sale! We're talking panic here....it was while they were eating and drinking and

Get the Deed! "Subject-To" the Existing Financing

barbecuing, came a knock on the front door that left them in shock. With mouths wide open and deep-fried chicken wing stuck between their teeth... Oh, Shhht one of them said reading the big, thick wad of papers just handed to them.... I could go on and on with this story, but you get the picture.

Typically, sellers who are over-leveraged (upside down) or have very little equity have a hard time selling their properties. In fact, quite often and you don't have to look too hard, you'll find nice, newer homes are completely vacant, the owner has gone and all you can hear are the crickets...they are nowhere to be found. When you check it out you will see that they didn't own it more than two years and there is no equity, and they are over leveraged. That's why some people walk away, especially in California where the owner-occupied borrower has no liabilities and can walk away, not so for some especially higher end borrowers with jumbo loans. Why bother to list it when there's nothing to get or worst, come out of pocket and pay a Realtor® commission out of pocket. Real estate agents won't list a home like this unless they can get a short sale approval from the lender or the seller comes out of pocket to pay the short fall plus their commission.

As the investor, this means big profits for you. The way the Subject-To investor approaches this situation is, we reason

Get the Deed! "Subject-To" the Existing Financing

and say it doesn't make sense to get a new mortgage and paying closing costs to buy a property with little or no equity. However, it becomes a much better deal when you can step in, take over payments with nothing down and nothing out of your pocket. The process is fast and flexible and serves both the investor, the seller and even the lender.

As you reach out to sellers, you will undoubtedly find that seller who is going through foreclosure and is in way over their heads in what is called the pre foreclosure process. They have missed a few payments and the lender has called the loan due and will take away the house if the loan isn't made whole. I like working with sellers in the notice stage, that's before a judgment or sale date has been entered. During this time there's a lot of emotions flying around, they are mad at themselves, the bank and their spouse for letting the house go into foreclosure. These ones, I like when they call me because by the time, they reach out to me, they've decided that they need my help. I explain to everyone that what I have to do is "surgery" so don't call me unless you're prepared for my sub2 offer.

Working with sellers in foreclosure is different from regular sellers and should be approached with care and caution, you really need some training before you step into this ring. Although you don't need money to do these deals, you can still get clobbered and end up wasting your time and theirs. But

Get the Deed! "Subject-To" the Existing Financing

ooohh! these deals are sweet, this is where I make the largest chunks of cash, man I feel like badass, black catsuit and cape!! Rock and roll baby. I was definitely feeling empowered and finally in control of my life, badass, yeah!

As of the date of this book, I just finished working with a seller in LA. A higher end house of 9 bedrooms and 9 baths siting on just under an acre. They were out of state owners and had almost stopped making payments. Every month payments were sent late and that took a major toll on their credit rating, FICO score plummeted from 700's to 400's so that they could not refinance their property, and this stopped them from doing most anything else. You see people on that price level need their credit and doing a short sale was out of the question. This lender just kept selling and assigning the mortgage note, just going from lender to lender. Each one would put it in foreclosure and start the process with a Notice of Default (NOD) and then just leave it there only to later cancel the NOD. Finally, the last lender set a date and posted a Notice of Sale on the front door of the occupied property. That's when they called me. The AS IS value is only around $800,000 and the amount owed is $700,000, not really over-leveraged. The bank kept giving them extensions and did not want to foreclose probably because they would have had a hard time re-selling, not sure but the crazy tenants had their goats and chickens in the back yard.

Get the Deed! "Subject-To" the Existing Financing

I simply negotiated a loan modification taking advantage of the lender's inability to foreclose. It was easy because it seemed that there were some reasons why they did not want to or could not foreclose…..probably because of those goats!

.

Get the Deed! "Subject-To" the Existing Financing

Get the Deed! "Subject-To" the Existing Financing

Frequently Asked Questions

You're probably wondering a whole lot of things right now, thinking everything said was definitely have.

What would happen if the bank found out that the original borrower is not making the payments? Listen, the bank doesn't care who makes the payments or from whom the checks are coming, just as long as the payments are being made and they get their money.

Who pays the taxes or takes the tax deductions? You do, you own it, you pay for it, you are in total control, you have the deed to the property.

Who has Personal Liability? You should talk to a lawyer to answer this question. Based on common knowledge, you are liable for the real estate since you own the property but not for the loan. Since you are not formally assuming the mortgage loan, meaning not going through a formal assumption where you have to apply and qualify for a mortgage. There is really no personal liability on your part. The loan stays in the sellers' name until you pay it off. Even though there is no personal liability, you must make

Get the Deed! "Subject-To" the Existing Financing

the payments if you want to keep the property, otherwise you and the seller both lose.

Why would a seller sign over their house Subject-To the existing mortgage? The general feel of the transaction is calm and stress free and the seller is usually very happy once the deal is done. The general disposition of the seller is different from normal, the situation is most likely a distressed situation. In the case you are simply making an offer to take over payments and release the seller from his financial obligation. This is not a formal assumption, it's an alternative. The bigger goal should be to help improve the seller's credit. Usually when you approach a distressed seller, he is frequently in arrearage on some of his bills therefore his credit is not so good. If you think of it, you are an angel sent to help the borrower and the lender. In effect you have stopped, prevented a foreclosure, paid the arrearages and reinstated the loan. As you begin to make regular payments the seller's credit will improve and the lender's loss is minimized and bypass a foreclosure. You have set him up for the future as his credit score will improve and he will be able to buy again.

How many houses can I buy? The short answer is ….all of them! You're not limited as the number of properties you can buy. If you were buying the conventional way with a mortgage, lenders will but a restriction on the number of properties you have mortgaged and that will put a ceiling on your business. One of the challenges we investors face is the amount of financing we can get. As your portfolio grows, you will be constricted and your buying power will be less and less, your investment goals will be weakened and that could put a stop to your business fast. Buying properties Subject-To the mortgage eliminate the credit limit problem and keeps your credit report clean.

Is this a relatively new technique?

In fact, it is not. Investors were buying houses in the 80's like hotcakes taking over mortgages subject-to. As of late, it seems like only a few experienced investors that are using this technique. It's a secret they don't want you to find out. Most investors don't know about buying subject-to that's why there is not much competition.

What if I can't make the payments?

If you're starting out like I did, you will understand the pain I went through, could not qualify for anything. Even so, you can still make money in real estate. You are in effect borrowing someone else's credit to own a property, using Other People's Mortgages, OPM. This is a serious thing; you must be respectable of your sellers credit and be sure to make those payments on time and do as you've agreed. DO NOT make the mistake of ruining someone else's credit, it would be better to just turn around and sell the property rather than cause the property to go through foreclosure.

What do I need to set up this business?

All you need is a desk, calculator, computer, lockbox, business card and an LLC. Use a spare room, a part of the garage or your kitchen table. Use an area where you can store all your equipment and paperwork.

What kind of business structure should I use?

You can choose to operate under certain legal structure, there are advantages and disadvantages of all. My personal recommendation would be an LLC registered in your state. I've found that an LLC provides better asset protection and requires very limited paperwork for filing and maintaining your business status. When you take over properties, you will do business under this LLC name.

What is Legal Possession?

It has to do with who legally is in possession that could be a tenant or the owner. A tenant has legal possession through an agreement called a lease or rental agreement. The owner does not need any agreement to take possession only in the case where the tenant exits, and the owner takes back legal possession. In the "subject-to" transaction, the buyer (YOU) will get both.

Is a Note & Mortgage the same?

The loan is the existing debt incurred by the seller that is left in place, it is also called the promissory note. The "note" consists of a promissory note which you don't see filed in public records and the Deed of Trust or Mortgage instrument is filed in public records. The mortgage or the deed of trust tells of the note and of the property that is encumbered. The promissory note is a security instrument that is serviced or maintained by the lender. The promissory note (the note) can be sold and transferred from investor to investor. These investors operate on the secondary mortgage market. The borrower will continue to make payments under the same terms and conditions as to the original lender. The note investor has no limits as to how many times they can sell and transfer their note. Only the borrower is limited in the transfer of his property under his mortgage because of his agreement.

Who are the mortgagor and the mortgagee?

The borrower is the mortgagor, and the lender is the mortgagee. The correct legal term is the borrower *gives* a mortgage to the lender in order to borrow money in order to buy real estate. The lender, who is the mortgagee holds the lien against the property.

Get the Deed! "Subject-To" the Existing Financing

Epilogue

Deal Killers, When You Have to Back Out

The thought of taking over properties Subject-To their mortgage is delicious and is the best financing strategy I've found, there most certainly are clear benefits. However, there are risks that must be understood.

The Due on Sale Clause. Yes, the lender has the right to and can call that loan due if they find out that the borrower has passed title and there is another owner on title. However, it does not usually happen and most of the time the lender is happy that someone else is willing to take over and keep the loan out of default.

Over-Leveraged Properties – there are too many of these in the marketplace and you'll definitely find a few of these. The thing to remember is that is what makes the deals so great. There is almost no competition, most real estate investors just pass these by, so there is lots of room for deal creation and more income for you.

Seller Interference. There could be some seller interference whereby the seller has not moved on. They keep rubber necking to see what you're up to and what is happening to the property.

Get the Deed! "Subject-To" the Existing Financing

These problems mean that you have not done a good job of closing the seller. It takes practice to get things humming in a system. This is not a problem at all if you handle with care and respect.

Title Insurance. The title could be a mess and you won't know if you don't check. So, for your sake, CHECK THE TITLE before you buy. Simple title search can be done using your favorite title company or search companies online. You will not necessarily have to buy new title, but you should at least check the title.

Overall, the rewards are greater than the risks when purchasing Subject-To and you can achieve financial freedom just taking over mortgages and renting the properties. You won't need any money to start and you're helping people. I didn't cover everything here, but I try to do that on my YouTube channel.

Sometimes you have to back out.

As with anything, you don't want to make any investment unless you check it out first. How do you perform due diligence in subject-to transactions? First due diligence is a major step in the process, it has to do with a thorough review of the condition of the property, verifying the information on the loan, checking the status of the loan, checking any unpaid tax and other liens

Get the Deed! "Subject-To" the Existing Financing

recorded against the property. The investor must perform due diligence to his satisfaction before closing the deal.

Sometimes you have to just say no and walk away. I recently found a deal in Los Angeles where the seller couldn't sell his home and was selling it himself. I found him on Craigslist. When I checked it out, he wasn't over-leveraged and wasn't in foreclosure or bankruptcy, as a matter of fact he had some equity but was asking too much. I finally struck a deal and was getting ready to close. As customary before closing, I always performed my due diligence, and it was a good thing I did. I was trying to get a property inspection done when I notice the seller was reluctant to letting me have access to the property it was vacant and I couldn't see the big deal why he was reluctant. He kept dodging my request and talking around my direct questions.

Finally, I insisted, and I went to the property to see what was going on. The noise from the front door was so loud that I had to look in and see for myself what was going on. I peeked in and to my surprise… what did I see? A huge snake thing, the noise was loud as it was the high-powered blower designed to dry out very wet places, this was no fan! Then I noticed holes in the walls, like someone had deliberately knocked out the drywall. Of course, you guessed it he had a flood, a really bad water damage, seemed that water was everywhere. As you can guess I backed out of the deal immediately and tore up the

Get the Deed! "Subject-To" the Existing Financing

contract! First, I make it a point not to deal with dishonest people, the guy was going to let me buy without knowing that there were problems. Second, the repairs would have cost me more than the minimum I would want to make $20K. Third, fixers are not really my thing anyway, so I stayed away.

It's important to say that while outsiders look at investors as the thieves, that's not really true, it's the dishonest sellers we really need to watch out for. Don't think it's all on you to prove yourself trustworthy, watch out for the desperate sellers as well.

Next Steps....

Hopefully I've given you a better idea of how Subject-To works and how you too can buy and sell real estate Subject-To the underlying financing. I couldn't teach you everything here but there is a lot more information on my website and on my YouTube channel. Please take a minute to do the following steps....

Step 1. Please take a minute to write a positive review on Amazon letting me know if you have learned from this book. Leave a positive review for this book by visiting the amazon.com books review page.

Step 2. Visit my YouTube channel and subscribe. You'll find free educational interaction and information on how to start and profit from investing in real estate using the Subject-To technique.

Step 3. Visit the Get the Deed Subject-To course website and claim your FREE trial. If you want to get trained, please don't hesitate to take the class, all forms and support are included.

Let's stay in touch. To Your Success ☺

Learn how to become a real estate investor at

www.MyCashFlowUniversity.com

YouTube.com/c/AliciaCoxMedia

APPENDIX A

Real Estate Investor Associations

Arizona

Arizona REIA Inc.

http://azreia.org/

AZREIA - Tuscon

http://azreia.org/

California

LA South REIA

http://lasouthreia.com/

Los Angeles Real Estate Investors Group
LAREIA

Prosperity Through Real Estate

http://www.prosperitythroughrealestate.com/

San Diego

San Diego Creative Investors Assoc.

http://sdcia.com/

Colorado

Investment Community of the Rockies Denver

7120 E Orchard Road Ste 400

Centennial, CO 80111

www.icorockies.com/

Connecticut

Connecticut REIA

PO BOX 270896

W Hartford, 06127

www.ctreia.com

Florida

Marion County REIA (MC-REIA)

3101 SW 34th Ave. #905-144

Ocala, FL 34474

www.mcreia.net/

Marion County REIA (MC-REIA)

Get the Deed! "Subject-To" the Existing Financing

3101 SW 34th Ave. #905-144
Ocala, FL 34474
www.mcreia.net

Central Florida Realty investors Association
www.cfri.net/

Broward REIA
www.breia.com

Georgia
North Metro Real Estate Investors Association
www.northmetroreia.com

Illinois
Metro East REIA
3 Eagle Ctr Suite 3
O'Fallon, IL 62269
www.metroeastreia.com

Springfield Area Landlord Association (SALA
www.salaonline.com
Chicago Creative Investors Association
PO Box 495

Glen Ellyn, IL 60137

www.ccia-info.com

Indiana

REIA of North Central Indiana

www.reia-nci.org

Kansas

Mid-America Association of Real Estate Investors

www.marei.org

Kentucky

Kentuckiana REIA

PO BOX 91225

Louisville, KY 40291

kreia.com/

Louisiana

New Orleans REIA

neworleansreia.com

Maryland

Traction REIA - Maryland

www.tractionreia.com

Mid Atlantic Real Estate Investors Association
www.mareia.com/

Massachusetts
Northern Worcester County Landlord Association
www.nwcla.com

New England REIA
www.newenglandreia.com

Michigan
RPOA of Kent County
www.rpoaonline.org

Genesee Landlord Association
2540 S Grand Traverse
Flint, MI 48503
www.geneseelandlordassoc.org
Michigan REIA
www.michiganrealestateinvestors.com

Minnesota

Minnesota REIA
www.mnreia.com/

Nebraska
Omaha REIA
2420 N 147th St
Omaha, 68116

Nevada
REIA Las Vegas
http://reialv.com/

New Hampshire
NewHampshirereia.org
www.newhampshirereia.org

NHREIA
www.nhreia.com/

New Jersey
South Jersey REIA
sjreia.org

Metro REIA

www.mreia.com

Union, NJ

New Mexico

Albuquerque Congress on Real Estate

http://www.acrenm.com/

New York

Freedom 1st REIA, Ltd.

48 North Ave

Rochester, NY 14626

www.ffreia.com

REIA NYC

www.reianyc.org

Long Island Real Estate Investment Association

Middle Island, NY

www.lireia.com

East Coast REIA

PO BOX 268

Oakdale, NY 11769

www.eastcoastreia.net

North Carolina

Triad Real Estate Investors Association Inc

www.triadreia.org

Metrolina Real Estate Investors Association

6401 Carmel Road Suite 205

Charlotte, NC 28226

www.metrolinareia.com

Ohio

REIA of Toledo

www.toledoreia.com

Oklahoma

Oklahoma City Real Estate Investor Association

www.okcreia.com

Oregon

Northwest REIA

15532 SW Pacific Hwy PMB 312

Tigard, OR 97224

http://www.northwestreia.com/

Pennsylvania

ACRE of Pittsburgh, Inc
www.acrepgh.org

CARPOA
www.carpoa.org

REIA of Reading Berks
www.REIAberks.org/

Diversified Real Estate Investor Group
1250 Bethlehem Pike #S-391
Hatfield, PA 19440
www.digonline.org/

Delco Property Investors
P.O. Box 1812
Media, PA 19063
delcopropertyinvestors.com/

Rhode Island

Rhode Island Real Estate Investors Group
www.rireig.com

Tennessee

Real Estate Investors of Nashville

www.reintn.org

Memphis Investors Group

PO Box 3554

Cordova, TN 38088

www.memphisinvestorsgroup.com

Knoxville Real Estate Investors

7115 Rising Road

Knoxville, TN 3792

knoxreia.com/

Texas

Austin REIA

www.austinreia.org

Alamo REIA

www.alamoreia.org/

Dallas REIA

www.dallasreia.org/

Utah

Utah REIA
www.utahreia.org

Virginia
Tidewater Real Estate Investors Group (TRIG)
www.trigofva.com

Chesterfield REIA
www.chesterfieldreia.com/

Washington
Real Estate Association of Puget Sound
http://www.reapsweb.com

Wisconsin
Milwaukee REIA
www.milwaukeereia.com

Madison REIA
www.madisonreia.com/

Appleton REIA
www.appletonreia.com

Get the Deed! "Subject-To" the Existing Financing

APPENDIX B

Sample Ads

WE BUY HOUSES
and Take Over Payments
(000) 000-0000
www.yourwebsite.com

ALTERNATIVES TO FORECLOSURE
Don't lose out to foreclosure. We can help
(000) 000-0000
www.yourwebsite.com

RENT-TO-OWN
No Bank Qualifying
(000) 000-0000
www.yourwebsite.com

FOR SALE BY OWNER
OWNER WILL FINANCE
No Qualifying, No Banks, No Credit
(000) 000-0000
www.yourwebsite.com

Get the Deed! "Subject-To" the Existing Financing

APPENDIX
C

Forms

AUTHORIZATION TO RELEASE LOAN INFORMATION

Authorization dated this _____ day of _____, 20_____

Borrower(s): _____

Loan No.: _____

Property: _____

TO: _____
    _____
    _____

I/We the undersigned hereby authorize you to release information regarding the above-referenced loan to _____
and/or their agents/assigns. This form may be duplicated in blank and or sent via facsimile transmission. This authorization is a continuation authorization for said persons to receive information about my loan, including duplicates of any notices sent to me regarding my loan.

_____   DOB _____
Borrower
                                      SSN _____

_____   DOB _____
Borrower
                                      SSN _____

Get the Deed! "Subject-To" the Existing Financing

PROPERTY INFORMATION SHEET

OWNER INFORMATION
Date: _____ Lead Source: _____
Property Address: _____
_____
Contact Person: _____
Owner of Record: _____ Cell Phone: _____
Owner of Record: _____ Home Phone: _____
Mailing Address: _____ Work Phone: _____
Email: _____

PROPERTY DESCRIPTION
PROPERTY TYPE: ☐Condo ☐Single Family ☐Multi Family ☐Commercial
Parcel Number: _____
# of Bed: _____ Year Built: _____ SqFt: _____ HOA: _____
# of Bath: _____ Garage: _____ Lot Size: _____
# of Stories: _____ Fireplace: _____ # of Units: _____
Building Style: _____ Pool: _____ Zoning: _____
Special Features: _____

SALE INFORMATION
Date of Purchase: _____ Tax Assessed Value: _____ Tax Status: _____
Amount Paid: _____ Tax Amount: _____ Market Value: _____

PRICE & MOTIVATION
Is Property Occupied?: ☐Owner ☐Tenants ☐Vacant
Motivation: ☐Hot ☐Warm ☐Cold
Is there a particular reason for selling at this time? _____
How quickly are you looking to sell? _____
How much are you asking? _____ Are you flexible _____
How did you come up with that amount? _____
Is Property Leased? Rental Income: _____ Length of Lease: _____

MORTGAGE INFO
NEGOTIATION: ☐Loan Discount ☐Short Sale ☐Settlement
1st Mortgage $_____ IR %_____ ☐Fixed ☐Adj. Loan Type: ☐Jumbo ☐Conventional ☐FHA ☐VA
Balance: $_____ Monthly Payment (PITI): $_____ Last Payment Made: __/__/__
Servicer: _____ Tel. _____ Ext. _____ Fax. _____
Loan No.: _____ Social Sec No.: _____ Social Sec No.: _____
DEFAULT ☐Y ☐N TS#_____ # PYMTS behind _____ SALE DATE: __/__/__
2nd Mortgage $_____ IR %_____ ☐Fixed ☐Adj. Loan Type: ☐Jumbo ☐Conventional ☐FHA ☐HELOC
Balance: $_____ Monthly Payment (PITI): $_____ Last Payment Made: __/__/__
Servicer: _____ Tel. _____ Ext. _____ Fax. _____
Loan No.: _____ Social Sec No.: _____ Social Sec No.: _____
DEFAULT ☐Y ☐N TS#_____ # PYMTS behind _____ SALE DATE: __/__/__
Financial Hardship: ☐Filed Bankruptcy ☐Lost Job ☐Business Failure ☐Reduced Pay
Other Hardship: ☐ Illness ☐Death ☐Other: _____

REALTOR INFORMATION
Realtor _____ Phone _____ Date of Listing _____
MLS # _____ DOM _____ Listing Expires _____

REPAIRS
Repair Costs: $_____
Repairs: _____

About the Author

Alicia A. Cox is a licensed real estate broker and a seasoned real estate investor. Alicia.is an expert in creative real estate buying and selling strategies. Alicia earned her success through creatively buying and selling houses using no money and has successfully bought and sold numerous properties. Alicia is the broker of record at Homeward Realty Corporation, a real estate services company with offices in California and Texas.

Alicia has built other successful businesses in the past, an attorney support paralegal company, and a temporary paralegal help service company with offices in New York and New Jersey. Alicia held several government contracts from FDIC, NJ Transit, school districts, various large corporate firm and employed over 60 full time employees.

Get the Deed! "Subject-To" the Existing Financing

If you enjoyed learning about this topic…you may be interested in…

Get the Deed "Subject-To" The Existing Mortgage Course.

visit the course website at: www.MyCashFlowUniversity.com

Proudly Made in the USA

Oceanside, CA

Made in the USA
Middletown, DE
28 March 2021